WOMEN WHO WIN

Laila Ali

Cynthia Cooper

Lindsay Davenport

Mia Hamm

Martina Hingis

Chamique Holdsclaw

Marion Jones

Anna Kournikova

Michelle Kwan

Lisa Leslie

Gabrielle Reece

Dorothy "Dot" Richardson

Sheryl Swoopes

Venus & Serena Williams

CHELSEA HOUSE PUBLISHERS

WOMEN WHO WIN

Marion Jones

Vicki Cox

Introduction by
HANNAH STORM

CHELSEA HOUSE PUBLISHERS
Philadelphia

Frontis: Arms spread in victory, Marion celebrates her gold medal win in the women's 100-meter finals at the 2000 Olympics in Australia.

CHELSEA HOUSE PUBLISHERS

Editor in Chief: Sally Cheney
Director of Production: Kim Shinners
Production Manager: Pamela Loos
Art Director: Sara Davis
Production Editor: Diann Grasse

Staff for Marion Jones
Editor: Sally Cheney
Associate Editor: Benjamin Kim
Associate Art Director: Takeshi Takahashi
Layout by D&G Limited.

The Chelsea House World Wide Web address is
http://www.chelseahouse.com

First Printing

1 3 5 7 9 8 6 4 2

Library of Congress Cataloging-in-Publication Data

Cox, Vicki.
  Marion Jones / Vicki Cox.
   p. cm.—(Women who win)
Includes bibliographical references and index.
ISBN 0-7910-6533-2 (alk. paper)
  1. Jones, Marion, 1975—Juvenile literature. 2. Runners (Sports)—United
States—Biography—Juvenile literature. 3. Women runners—United
States—Biography—Juvenile literature. [1. Jones, Marion, 1975.
2. Track and field athletes. 3. African Americans—Biography.
4. Women—Biography.] I. Title. II. Series.

GV1061.15.J67 C69 2001
796.42'2'092—dc21
  [B]   2001028793

CONTENTS

WOMEN WHO WIN

Hannah Storm
NBC Studio Host

You go girl! Women's sports are the hottest thing going right now, with the 1900s ending in a big way. When the U.S. team won the 1999 Women's World Cup, it captured the imagination of all sports fans and served as a great inspiration for young girls everywhere to follow their dreams.

That was just the exclamation point on an explosive decade for women's sports—capped off by the Olympic gold medals for the U.S. women in hockey, softball, and basketball. All the excitement created by the U.S. national basketball team helped to launch the Women's National Basketball Association (WNBA), which began play in 1997. The fans embraced the concept, and for the first time, a successful and stable women's professional basketball league was formed.

I was the first ever play-by-play announcer for the WNBA—a big personal challenge. Broadcasting, just like sports, had some areas with limited opportunities for women. There have traditionally not been many play-by-play opportunities for women in sports television, so I had no experience. To tell you the truth, the challenge I faced was a little scary! Sometimes we are all afraid that we might not be up to a certain task. It is not easy to take risks, but unless we push ourselves we will stagnate and not grow.

Here's what happened to me. I had always wanted to do play-by-play earlier in my career, but I had never gotten the opportunity. Not that I was unhappy—I had been given studio hosting assignments that were unprecedented for a woman and my reputation was well established in the business. I was comfortable in my role . . . plus I had just had my first baby. The last thing I needed to do was suddenly tackle a new skill on national television and risk being criticized (not to mention, very stressed out!). Although I had always wanted to do play-by-play, I turned down the assignment twice, before reluctantly agreeing to give it a try. During my hosting stint of the NBA finals that year, I traveled back and forth to WNBA preseason games to practice play-by-play. I was on 11 flights in 14 days to seven different cities! My head was spinning and it was no surprise that I got sick. On the day of the first broadcast, I had to have shots just so I could go on the air without throwing up. I felt terrible and nervous, but I survived my first game. I wasn't very good but gradually, week by week,

I got better. By the end of the season, the TV reviews of my work were much better—*USA Today* called me "most improved."

During that 1997 season, I witnessed a lot of exciting basketball moments, from the first historic game to the first championship, won by the Houston Comets. The challenge of doing play-by-play was really exciting and I loved interviewing the women athletes and seeing the fans' enthusiasm. Over one million fans came to the games; my favorite sight was seeing young boys wearing the jerseys of female players—pretty cool. And to think I almost missed out on all of that. It reinforced the importance of taking chances and not being afraid of challenges or criticism. When we have an opportunity to follow our dreams, we need to go for it!

Thankfully, there are now more opportunities than ever for women in sports (and other areas, like broadcasting). We thank women, like those in this series, who have persevered despite lack of opportunities—women who have refused to see their limitations. Remember, women's sports has been around a long time. Way back in 396 B.C. Kyniska, a Spartan princess, won an Olympic chariot race. Of course, women weren't allowed to compete, so she was not allowed to collect her prize in person. At the 1996 Olympic games in Atlanta, Georgia, over 35,600 women competed, almost a third more than in the previous Summer Games. More than 20 new women's events have been added for the Sydney, Australia, Olympics in 2000. Women's collegiate sports continues to grow,spurred by the 1972 landmark legislation Title IX, which states that "no person in the United States shall, on the basis of sex, be excluded from participation in, be denied the benefits of, or be subjected to discrimination under any educational program or activity receiving federal financial assistance." This has set the stage for many more scholarships and opportunities for women, and now we have professional leagues as well. No longer do the most talented basketball players in the country have to go to Europe or Asia to earn a living.

The women in this series did not have as many opportunities as you have today. But they were persistent through all obstacles, both on the court and off. I can tell you that Cynthia Cooper is the strongest woman I know. What is it that makes Cynthia and the rest of the women included in this series so special? They are not afraid to share their struggles and their stories with us. Their willingness to show us their emotions, open their hearts, bare their souls, and let us into their lives is what, in my mind, separates them from their male counterparts. So accept this gift of their remarkable stories and be inspired. Because you, too, have what it takes to follow your dreams.

1

DREAM CHASER

I want to be an Olympic Champion." Erasing her home-work assignments, Marion Jones printed that seven-word sentence on the blackboard in her bedroom. She was just 8 years old then. Her hair was in ponytails. Her bangs curled toward a smile that could light up a baseball dia-mond. She had just watched the torch relay en route to the Los Angeles 1984 Olympics. Behind her flashing black eyes, her dream was born.

Sixteen years later, Marion Jones entered Stadium Australia in Sydney, ready to make her dream come true. She was determined to make the 2000 Olympics her moment to win a gold medal in the 100-meter race.

One hundred thousand people had filled the stadium to watch her. The spectators wore colors of their own coun-tries. On their baseball caps, they pinned souvenirs of the 27th Olympiad. Some carried flags to wave when their favorites won. Their cameras flashed like glitter around the double-decker stadium. Their cheers and applause at other events in progress scattered like confetti across the night.

Wrapped in the stars and stripes, Marion takes her victory lap after winning the 100-meter run to earn Olympic gold.

Striding onto the track and slipping out of her warm up clothes, Marion Jones was no longer a soft, sweet, little third-grader. Tall, confident, and poised, she could just as easily have been a Greek goddess or Roman gladiator, stepping from a marble pedestal.

From her silver shoes to her tightly braided hair, every inch of her 5-foot 10-inch body was sculpted for speed. Long, muscled calves waited to unleash their energy. Her trademark biker shorts, in American royal blue, stretched over powerful thighs. Her abdomen and arms were bare in the evening breeze. They were smooth and sleek, pared of every ounce that could catch the wind and slow her down for a hundredth of a second.

Marion had been up most of the night before, thinking about this moment. Other athletes and spectators milled about Olympic Village, buying souvenirs, taking pictures, and laughing. But Marion and her husband, C.J. Hunter, stayed in their apartment in a suburb just outside Sydney. She repeatedly reviewed what she would have to do during each phase of the race. Early in the morning, C.J. had fixed breakfast. Then Marion met with Trevor Graham, her loyal friend and coach, for one last practice and workout. All the thinking and training were over now.

Marion waved politely at a television camera before turning off her dazzling beauty-queen smile. It was time for her competitor's face— intense, focused, dead serious. She had a dream to chase. It was time to do it.

Long forgotten were all the interviews and questions about her plans to win five gold medals in a single Olympics. It was a big undertaking, more medals than legendary

Olympians, Jesse Owens, Carl Lewis, and Florence Griffith Joyner had won. Forgotten, too, were the ten other races and nine long jumps she would enter over the next few days. She gave no thought to the glamorous photo shoots for *Vogue* and *People's Weekly*, and the commercials for Nike, Gatorade, and General Motors. She ignored the crowd's shouts and cheers and the helicopter swirling above the stadium.

She didn't see Australian Tatiana Grigorieva and American Stacy Gragila arc through the first Olympic women's pole-vaulting contest in another part of the stadium. She wasn't aware of the stadium's big screen or the officials in their navy jackets and ties. She took no notice of the photographers and their big-lensed cameras or the television camera on its rolling dolly along the sideline.

Each competitor from Jamaica, Bahamas, the Ukraine, and Greece wanted to put the gold medal around her own neck. But these world-class runners weren't really important to Marion, either. Her race was with the clock.

The world of Marion Jones narrowed between the white boundary lines of lane number five. Straight down that red track, the finish line waited 100 meters away.

Marion bent forward, letting her arms dangle, fingers nearly touching the ground. She stretched out. She jiggled both legs. She gave them one last quick massage with her fists.

It was time.

"Take your marks," said an official.

She carefully placed her left foot against the forward starting block, her right foot against the back block.

"Set," the official said.

Marion rounds the final turn in the women's 200-meter run at the 2000 Olympics in Sydney, Australia. The 200-meter sprint was a favorite of Marion's, and she won the event easily.

She spread her fingers into little tripods behind the starting line and leaned slightly forward. She had to react—react instantly—to the sound of the starter gun. Move the right leg and left hand forward—immediately. A good start was critical. The race would be over in less than 11 seconds.

"When the gun goes off, I go, Boom!" Marion said of a race's beginning.

After hours of training and dozens of races, everything was automatic for Marion. Drive out of the starting blocks. Hurdle all body weight forward. Keep the head low. Look at your shoes. Don't pop up too early. Begin the cycling motion; drive the knees up. Keep the feet under the body. Relax. Run straight up. Don't lean forward at the finish line.

Marion's powerful legs coiled. Her determination tightened. She waited for the starting gun. Another runner broke the tension, asking an official to have everyone stand up in the runner's blocks. After complying, the runners repositioned themselves. Then Ekaterina Thanou of Greece, just to the left of Marion's lane, anticipated the gun and false started. Everyone waited until she returned to the starting line. The athletes again tightened their concentration and reset themselves in their blocks, again. Marion took one final look down her lane. Her eyes turned deadly. Slowly she lowered her head, licked her lips, and waited.

The gun cracked. Marion unleashed her energy—perfectly. Leaning forward, she accelerated with every step. Each stride stretched further and further. Her knees pumped up and down, reaching, slicing through the space before them.

At ten meters, barely a second into the race, Marion was already ahead of everyone else. All her muscles worked together flawlessly. Her legs and arms pumped in a smooth rhythm. Right leg with left hand. Left leg with right hand. Her hands were a blur, slashing through the air. Her feet barely touched the ground. Her expression, unlike those of the other runners, was relaxed and empty of strain. At 30 meters, her head was straight up, transitioning to her full-out running position. By 50 meters, a mere 5 seconds after the gun fired, she had reached full speed. Her eyes, focused on the finish line, did not flinch.

"It's like somebody has a rubber band attached to me, and they just let go," Marion said.

Arms and legs, still paired in opposites, moved in unison, slicing through the air. Her feet skimmed the track surface. No one could catch her. She was running alone.

At 90 meters, she passed the Olympic logo on the track fence and the cameraman kneeling on the infield. She couldn't hear the others breathing. She couldn't hear their feet thud against the track. She knew she had won. She flung her arms open and spread her fingers, as if to gather in every thousandth second of the victory. A step later, she crossed the finish line, laughing. She hopped, tapped her chest, and pumped a fist into the air. Then the fastest woman in the world dropped to the track and did something she seldom does. She cried.

Marion hadn't expected to do that. After all, she had won every 100-meter race she had started in for the last three years. She had won in the United States. She had won in Europe. She had won in Asia. But this was the Olympic Games.

"I was like 'I was going to cross that line and be a cool cat,'" she said. "And then all of a sudden you realize you can be described—finally—as an Olympic champion. It's very emotional." She found Trevor Graham, her mother Marion Toler, and her brother Albert in the stands. Surrounded by television cameramen, they were clapping and smiling and laughing. C.J., all 330 pounds of him, was jumping up and down, yelling, and smiling.

"At first, all I felt was joy," Marion said. "But when I looked over and saw my family, I just lost it."

Running over to them, she grabbed the American flag and the flag of Belize, her mother's native country. She draped the American flag like a cape over her back and circled the track in a victory lap. She waved. Her famous smile, her crooked tooth, and her dancing eyes charmed the spectators. The crowd, knowing it had seen the beginning of Olympic history, cheered and waved back.

"This is 19 years of trying and dreaming, of working out on those tough days, those cold days," she said. "It all comes down to one moment and one race."

She climbed onto the winner's stand, still smiling and waving. Fastened to a sea-blue ribbon was the object of her dreams. She bent down so the official could place the gold medal around her neck. Then she picked it up, examined it, and set it back down against her chest.

"I always imagined what it would look like," she later said. "There's no rough edges. It's very smooth. It's very glamorous, I think. It's beautiful."

It took Marion Jones 10.75 seconds to earn her first Olympic gold medal. Her time was just 11 one-hundredths behind Florence Griffith Joyner's Olympic record. In the largest margin of victory since 1952, Marion had run so fast, the rest of the field trailed seven meters, two bicycle lengths, behind her. They knew they never really had a chance. "I was running only for the silver," Ekaterina Thanou admitted after the race.

On one cool September evening in the first Olympics of the new millennium, Marion Jones had really raced only the wind. After 16 years and three Olympiads, a little girl's wish had come true. She held an Olympic gold medal in her hand. Who could blame her if she kissed it? Her grown-up ambition to win four more golds had yet to follow.

2

"HARD NAILS"

Watching the televised marriage of Lady Diana and Prince Charles, five-year-old Marion Jones asked her mother about the red carpet the Royal Couple walked.

Told only important people could use it, Marion replied, "Well, when I go places, why don't they roll it out for me?"

Marion was born confident. She wasn't afraid of the dark or of snakes. She thought she could do anything her brother, Albert, and his friends did. Once they discovered she could, they nicknamed her "Hard Nails."

"She could dribble a basketball, run races with us, ride bikes with us. She could throw a baseball and hit one. When it came to games, she didn't have any girl-like qualities," recalls Albert, who is five years older than Marion. "She was strong, almost as tall as most of my friends, and she never, ever quit."

Marion, Albert, their mother, and stepfather lived in Palmdale, a Los Angeles suburb. Her mother had overcome a difficult childhood in the Central American country of Belize. "Big Marion's" marriage to Albert's father, Albert Kelly, had failed. Her marriage to Marion's father, George Jones, lasted only four years.

In perfect form, Marion bolts down the track in the women's 100-meter sprint. With short runs as her strongest events, Marion outdistances the rest of the field in a flash.

Big Marion and George were never happy together. By the time "Little Marion" was born, October 12, 1975, George was disappearing and reappearing without a word. When he vandalized their Beverly Hills home one day, Marion's mother divorced him. He wanted nothing to do with Marion. That hurt Marion for a long time.

"The fact that I have no past on my father's side, nothing of my father's family heritage or who they were or where they were from, is like a missing link in my mind," she said, "And in my heart."

But Ira Toler, whom Big Marion married in 1983, was completely different. Marion's stepfather loved her very much, and she adored him. "Whenever he went somewhere, whether it was to the store or to the lodge to hang out with his buddies, I'd be right there," Marion recalled. "It was almost like I was living in his back pocket."

A retired postal worker, Ira stayed home while Marion's mother worked as a legal secretary around Los Angeles. He helped Marion with her homework and cooked her favorite meal, macaroni and cheese. Sometimes he surprised her at school with a cheeseburger and fries for lunch.

Ira, Big Marion, and Albert were drawn into Marion's constant energy. Ira drove Marion to T-ball and gymnastics practice. Albert took her on his bicycle to ballet lessons. Big Marion critiqued athletes' interviews as she and Marion watched them on television. Already running competitive track by age ten, Marion was often interviewed herself.

In 1987 Ira died unexpectedly of a stroke. At twelve, Marion was left again without a strong male figure in her life.

"Losing Ira was tough," she says. "I dealt with it the way I usually do. I bottled up my feelings."

Marion turned to running. Now working two jobs to support her family, Big Marion helped. The family moved from suburb to suburb around Los Angeles, seeking outstanding sports programs for Marion's athletic talents.

At Pinecrest Junior High, Marion's potential was obviously beyond neighborhood fun and games. "I felt confident that she could be an Olympian," said one coach. By 1989 the eighth grader was sprinting the 100-meter race in 12.01 seconds, the 200-meter race in 24.06, and the 400-meter in 56.73.

Relocated near Rio Mesa High School, Marion caught another coach's attention. Noticing the spring in her legs and her quickness, Al Walker challenged her to touch the bottom of the basketball net. Marion jumped. Whisk! Could she slap the backboard? No problem. Marion jumped. Whap! Then he asked if she could reach the rim, ten feet above the floor. Marion circled the free-throw area and sprang into the air. Her hands rose past the net and grabbed the rim itself.

Rio Mesa's new basketball star averaged 24.5 points and 11 rebounds a game her first season. By spring, Rio Mesa's new track star could outrun almost anyone, girl or boy, on the track. Her times were constantly improving. In her first competition with athletes from outside the area in 1990, Marion met Inger Miller, already an established high school track star. They began a rivalry that would continue throughout their careers. That night Inger won both their 100-meter and 200-meter competitions by a single step. "It's a good thing you

Concentration before a race is vital to any winner. Here, Marion gets focused as she steps into the starting blocks for the 400-meter run at the Mt. San Antonio College Relays.

beat her now," a track official told Inger, "because I don't think you will ever beat her again." Who would've guessed he was right?

During Marion's sophomore year, she won the California High School State meet, the 100- and 200-meter dashes in the USA Junior meet, and was named 1991 High School Athlete of the Year. Her personal bests, 11.17 in the 100 and 22.76 in the 200, were world-class times. *Track and Field News* ranked the fifteen-year-old tenth nationwide in the 100 meters and in the top five in the 200. Nothing stopped her except the opportunities Rio Mesa offered. At year's end, she and her mother decided Marion should transfer again. Though her friends were at Rio Mesa, the level of competition at Thousand Oaks High School was higher.

"Sports outweighed everything else," Marion said. "Many times, students transfer because of an academic problem. My problem was with sports. My mom saw my eyes light up when I was going to a track meet or to a basketball game. I was a different person when it came time for sports."

By running track and playing basketball, Marion breathed, ate, and slept athletics year round. Her first major injury taught her how empty her life was without sports. In a basketball game with Simi Valley, Marion grabbed the ball and ran toward her basket. An opposing player could have tried to block Marion's shot or find a way to guard her. But with one of the country's fastest runners headed toward her full speed, the Simi Valley player turned her back to Marion and simply ducked. Marion couldn't stop. Her knee hit the player in the back, and she somersaulted over her. Marion landed on her wrist, breaking it in two places, and then hit the floor hard with her chin, dislocating her jaw.

Marion couldn't practice or compete. Waiting to heal, she couldn't do anything she loved to do. Depressed and irritable, she frequently argued with her mother.

"Marion was miserable," her mother said. "I stopped working, stayed home to nurse her, cook for her, help her get around, but still felt I couldn't do anything for her. She didn't want me to."

Others worried about Marion's two-sport interests. They feared injuries in either one could end her promising athletic career entirely. They were also fearful that the intensity of year-round competition could make her sick of all sports. They didn't know "Hard Nails" very well.

With the cast off her arm, Marion's priorities snapped back into place. She even canceled her date to a dance when a basketball playoff game was scheduled the same night. She finished the basketball season and was named an All County and All State player.

She then stepped into track season with her own personal style, beginning with the short shorts many female competitors hated. Marion refused to wear them even to practice, preferring longer Spandex bicycle shorts.

"All my life I saw these women wearing briefs, and always they gotta pull 'em out of their butt," she later said. "What's the point? Anyway, if briefs are so great, why aren't the men wearing them?"

She was noticed more for her new personal bests in both the 100 and 200 meters. Her time in the 200 meters, 22.58, set an American Junior record. She was named High School Athlete of the Year again. *Track and Field News* ranked her nationally in both the 100- and 200-meter races.

More publicity followed at the 1992 Olympic Trials in New Orleans. Her 200-meter time, 22.58 seconds, established a high school record that still stands. But missing third place in the 100-meter sprint by seven one-hundredths of a second, she qualified only as an alternate in the 4x100 relay team. As a member of the team, the 16-year-old would have automatically received any medal that the team won in Barcelona, Spain, whether she raced or not.

"I want to be an Olympic champion," she said. " . . . but when I'm eighty years old . . . and my grandkids run up to me, I want to be

000 U.S. OLYMPIC TEAM TRIALS | 2000 U.S. OLYMPIC TEAM TRIALS
'ACK AND FIELD SACRAMENTO | TRACK AND FIELD SACRAMENTO

able to show them my gold medals and say, 'See this, honey? This is something that I ran for, that I sweated for, that I earned. Nobody handed me this.'"

Marion Jones stayed home.

In 1993, during Marion's senior year, she encountered for the first time two controversies that would continue through her track career. First, while experimenting with other events—the shot put, hurdles, and high jump, among others—she discovered the long jump. It seemed simple enough. Run as fast as you can down the runway. Take off behind the foul line. Sail through the air the length of two living rooms, and land in the sand.

"I didn't know what the heck I was doing," recalls Marion of her first attempts. Experts instantly recognized her ability, but shuddered

After experimenting with other track and field events, including the hurdles and shot put, Marion tried her luck at the long jump, relying on her grit and determination often to guide her to victory in the event. Here she sails through the air at the 2000 U.S. Track and Field Trials.

as she propelled herself through the air, flailing her arms and legs. Marion, however, was hooked. Her speed and determination often helped her to win the event. Her long jump mark of 22 1/2 feet at a state meet was just short of the national high school record.

Secondly, Marion was chosen for random drug testing, which is designed to monitor athletes for performance-enhancing drugs. The Athletics Congress (TAC), the U.S. track's governing body, suspended her for failing to show up for a drug test. In a post office mix-up, the letter instructing her to take the test never reached her or her coach. Assuming that she couldn't pass the test, the TAC banned Marion from both national and international competitions for four years.

Marion's appeal seemed hopeless until Johnnie Cochran stepped in. A lawyer once involved in the O.J. Simpson trial, Cochran reminded TAC officers that they hadn't used telephone information Marion had provided. When he threatened going to federal court, the committee overturned Marion's suspension. Marion's name was cleared. Charging no fee, Cochran said, "My greatest fulfillment will be seeing her win in Australia."

Marion's final state championships in June 1993 closed the books on her extraordinary high school career. Marion finished first in the 100 and 200 meters and in the long jump, clinching a total of nine championships in four years. In basketball, she led the Thousand Oaks Lancers to two California Interscholastic Foundation (CIF) Division I championships. She once scored 48 points in a single game.

She averaged 22.8 points and 14.7 rebounds a game. She was named CIF Player of the Year and the Most Valuable Player of Ventura County. "Hard Nails" could do just about anything.

3

"FLASH"

Hundreds of colleges wanted Marion. For four years they had been sending her letters, trying to convince her to enroll in their sports program. Many urged her to concentrate on track and give up basketball.

Marion knew what she wanted. Academically, she wanted a school with a good journalism program. Athletically, she wanted scholarships in both basketball and track with the option to "red shirt" basketball her junior year to concentrate full-time on the U.S. Olympic Trials. When the University of North Carolina agreed, Marion became a Lady Tar Heel.

"I loved track, and I wanted to keep it like that," Marion said. "So many young runners get burned out, I figured I'd do both, but in the beginning, I needed discipline, and the Carolina basketball program is very structured."

Marion's mother moved with her, in part to watch over her daughter's best interests and in part just to watch her play ball. She hoped Marion would visit her and she could cook Marion's favorite dish of chicken and rice, flavored with Belize spices. But like any girl heading to college,

A woman of many talents. As a junior at the University of North Carolina, Marion served double duty, playing basketball for the Lady Tar Heels while preparing for the 1996 Olympics.

Marion wanted to be on her own. Although she found her mother in the crowd before a basketball game, gave her a kiss, and said a few words, she never visited her mother's apartment.

"I had always been independent, but when I went to college that was multiplied ten times. My mother and I butted heads a lot," Marion recalls.

Coach Sylvia Hatchell knew the talented freshman would be wasted sitting on the bench. With three returning players, the Lady Tar Heels didn't need Marion under the basket where her height usually put her. Hatchell made Marion the point guard, the player who ran the team and made decisions on the floor.

"Marion has a focus on what she wants to do like no one I've ever seen," Hatchell said. "She lets no one and nothing interfere. And she's so coachable. She'd watch films, ask questions. Whatever you showed her, she would perfect it. She was like a sponge."

Marion worked 45 extra minutes each day on her passing and dribbling. She learned to scan the whole court and make quick decisions. She could press more than 200 pounds. She enjoyed practicing with women who wanted to win as badly as she did. Sometimes they even practiced with the men's basketball team.

"We loved coming to practice. We loved scrimmaging. We loved drills," says Marion. "I don't know if I'll ever find another bunch of players like that. It was wonderful."

Around the Chapel Hill campus, Marion hung out with her teammates. She and Tracy Reid cut up at parties, inventing a step routine they called the Hoop Phi dance. With musical tastes including "The Sound of Music" and Michael Jackson's "Thriller," Marion nicknamed Tracy Reid "Hard Core." With Tonya Cooper, Marion visited a tattoo parlor where she found the right symbol for her own nickname. Already called "Flash" for her basketball quickness and speed, Marion had a bolt of lightning and wings tattooed on the inside of her right ankle.

Basketball practices, however, were all business. The Lady Tar Heels had never won an Atlantic Coast Conference title during Coach Hatchell's tenure. A conference title meant an automatic berth in the NCAA tournament and a shot at being national champion. Every session started at center court as the Lady Tar Heels grasped hands and yelled "National Champions!" Marion and her teammates were determined to win.

"She intimidates when she walks on the court," said her coach. "And she brings everybody on her team up to her level because she refuses to drop to someone else's."

"Flash" set high standards. She averaged 4.1 rebounds, 2.8 assists, and 14.1 points per game. Her 111 steals set a freshman conference record. With Marion, the team won every game except two. Only the University of Virginia, their opponent for the conference championship, had beaten them.

"The intensity in Marion's eyes was like daggers going through my body," Hatchell said as the team waited in the locker room before the conference title game. "We hadn't even gone out to warm up yet, and she had tears rolling down her face."

Her teammate Sylvia Crawley saw Marion's look, too. "It was contagious. We wanted to win so bad it hurt."

The Lady Tar Heels did win the title—and kept on winning right through the NCAA tournament. The excitement of becoming the 1994 National Champions carried on for weeks with an on-campus parade, a trip to the White House, and a visit from North Carolina alumnus, Michael Jordan.

Marion's success in basketball exacted a high price from her track career. The NCAA tournament took up Marion's track practice time. Savoring the details of the Championship win made it difficult to concentrate on hard, demanding track practices.

"My heart wasn't in it," she admitted. Her times did not improve over her last season's statistics. At the NCAA Track Championships in Boise, Idaho, she finished second in the long jump, sixth in the 200 meters, and didn't make finals in the 100 meters. But Marion was stubborn. She hung on to track *and* basketball, telling the media, "I'll continue to do that because I love both sports."

Basketball during her sophomore year was another banner year. The Lady Tar Heels posted a 30-5 record, won the ACC tournament, and advanced to the Sweet Sixteen in the NCAA tournament. Wearing no. 20 on her Lady Tar Heels blue, Marion averaged 17.0 points per game bringing her two-season point total to a 1000 points. Her rebounds increased to 5 per game, her assists went to 4.5; and she stole 124 balls. She was Honorable Mention All-American by the Associated Press and First Team All-Atlantic Coast conference.

But again, Marion wasn't "Flash" on the track. She was really just a part-time track athlete, and part-time athletes don't win. At the ACC Championships, her long jump was only 20' 10 1/2. She was disqualified in the 100 meters for two false starts. She dropped out completely of the 200-meter final. At the NCAA

Four times the gold. Marion (right) with members of the women's 4 x 400-meter relay team proudly display their gold medals at the 2000 Olympics. Joining Marion (from left) are Jearl Miles-Clark, Monique Hennagan, and La Tasha Colander-Richardson.

Championships she placed just fourth in the long jump. Her future as a runner and jumper looked grim.

Marion had planned to concentrate complete-ly on track her junior year. School officials had agreed to let Marion take off the 1995–96 basket-ball season to prepare. She flew to California to train for the 1996 Olympics. Then in August, at Coach Hatchell's invitation, Marion joined the USA basketball team as point guard for the World University Games. Marion thought two weeks out of her track training wouldn't make much difference. She was very wrong. In a Colorado Springs scrimmage, she and another player dove for a ball. The other player landed on Marion, breaking her left foot.

With a two-inch screw in the bone and her foot in a cast, Marion carefully followed her "rehab" regimen, swimming, and riding a sta-tionery bike. There was still time. The Olympics were still possible. In January, with the frac-ture healed and thinking about the long jump, she bounced on a trampoline.

"I came down a little awkwardly and imme-diately felt a pop and heard a squeaking sound," Marion said.

She re-fractured the same bone in the same place, even bending the screw in her foot. A new cast, a new larger screw, and bone marrow from Marion's hip couldn't save Marion's dreams. The basketball season and the Olympics disappeared into the plaster.

Marion couldn't do what she wanted to do. She couldn't do what her friends were doing. She got depressed. She argued with her mother. She lost interest in her journalism studies. Her grades fell. She watched from the sidelines as her teammates struggled through a 13-14 losing season. Barely able to walk, the only thing she could do was go to the weight room to work on her upper body strength.

There, Marion Jones met C.J. Hunter. A quiet, 330-pound shot-put competitor, C.J. had won bronze in the 1995 World Championships, had his own agent, and a small contract with Nike. He was seven years older than Marion, separated from his wife and two children, and was part of the coaching staff. Marion liked his intelligence and the way he made her laugh.

"I saw a warmth that he didn't show to everybody," she says. "He makes the people he cares about feel really special. Sure, he's a big guy. A lot of people have preconceived ideas about size, but I went into the relationship open-minded. I tell people that the best way to describe C.J. is that he's a big teddy bear."

They went to dinner and the movies, despite policy forbidding coach-athlete dating. When the university demanded he either coach track or date Marion, C.J. promptly resigned.

"It was an easy call," he said later "It was not a big deal."

Her foot out of its cast, Marion returned to Lady Tar Heels basketball. The team again won the conference championship. Marion was named the tournament's Most Valuable Player. With an 18.6-point average for the season, she was named First Team All-American by Basketball America. The Lady Tar Heels played two games in the NCAA tournament, but were upset by George Washington University. After the game, Marion announced she was quitting basketball.

C.J. was blamed. He and "M.J." were inseparable, in love, and engaged to be married. Critics assumed he influenced her decision. After all, as a world-class athlete, his life revolved around track, working out, traveling to competitions, and preparing for the 1996 Olympics.

But Marion said, "I wanted to get back to track, which had been my first love as a child. For four years I'd been doing everything for everybody else. Now I was gonna do something for Marion."

She left basketball with a slam dunk. Three years as point guard, she had helped the Tar Heels finish 92-10, win every conference tournament game, and earn a NCAA Championship. Her career points totaled 1,716 points.

Graduating with a journalism degree and with a fistful of honors, Marion Jones laced on her track shoes as a full-time professional.

"No one was going to tell me I couldn't play basketball and run track at the same time," she says. "But I came to understand that I couldn't realize my Olympic dream without committing full-time."

4

SHE'S BACK

Marion had some work to do. Her bulked-up basketball weight had to go. Her body had to be reconditioned. Running up and down the basketball court was completely different from competing in track. "Just running around the track made me use muscles I hadn't used in four years," she said.

There was another problem. It was one thing to run fast with her feet. It was another thing to run smart with her head. Marion needed a coach. C.J. had been trying to be one, but he admitted, "That's the same as saying she wasn't being coached at all." To be fair, the often-criticized C.J. had helped Marion. Besides suggesting workout drills, icing down her legs and back when she was tired, and giving her moral support, he introduced her to two key people: his agent, Charlie Wells, and Trevor Graham.

Trevor was a silver medalist in the 1988 Olympics. He had been using his scientific opinions about training and competition strategies with a dozen other athletes at Paul Derr Field where Marion practiced. He saw her great speed.

Hard landing. Marion hits the sand at the end of the long jump.

"She was just so much more explosive than any woman I've seen since Florence Griffith Joyner," Trevor said. "She was still a little overweight from basketball and her technique needed work, but her talent and competitiveness was something that can't be taught."

C.J. talked with Trevor Graham and asked him how Marion could improve. Trevor suggested small adjustments about staying low out of the starting blocks and swinging her arms differently. The improvement was instantaneous.

"Why don't you coach her?" C.J. suggested. Trevor began working with her, explaining his theories and techniques of running.

"She was picking up everything I taught her immediately," Trevor said. "It was like she knew all along and was just waiting for someone to tell her to do it."

Marion and Trevor worked long and hard. There was so much to learn. Stay low. Keep your chin down. Pull into running position. Swing your arms like you're beating a drum. Move your feet like you're pedaling a bicycle. Run like you've been sprung from a rubber band. Don't lean at the finish line. Don't look at the clock.

Marion was willing to do the work. "I can't be satisfied unless I know I'm training harder than anybody else in the world," she said. Six days a week, four to five hours a day, she was either on the track or lifting weights. She strapped a harness on her shoulders and dragged a heavy sled down the track. She ran sprints. She practiced accelerating out of the starting blocks. At the end of the day she was completely exhausted.

Playing basketball had trained her to consider nine other players on the entire court. Her teammates depended on her, and their opponents tried to outsmart her. She had to refocus her concern to just one person and just one goal. After all, in the running lane, Marion was the only one there. On the flip side, participating on the basketball court had given her a mental vacation from track. Had she been concentrating on track day in and day out for fifteen years, she might have lost interest in it.

With C.J. and Trevor helping her, Marion dropped her 15 extra basketball pounds and picked up the technique. She entered the 1997 track season with tournaments in Florida and North Carolina. In Tennessee, she ran the 100 meters in 10.98 seconds.

"We knew that bigger things were going to happen than we initially had thought," said Marion of her first-ever time under eleven seconds. "I knew I was ready to do something special."

That something special occurred in June, just 12 weeks after she lumbered onto the track to make her comeback. At the U.S. National Championships in Indianapolis, Marion sped down the track in 10.97 seconds, becoming national champion in the 100 meters.

Her old rival from high school days, Inger Miller said, "We all knew she was fast. But we also knew it takes years to reach a high level. Everyone was shocked at how quickly she hit those times."

Her conquest of the long jump was more complicated. Marion had the speed to race down the runway. She had the heart to run as hard as she could. To win, she had to control where her foot landed at the end of the runway.

If she crossed the takeoff board, she would be disqualified, no matter how far she jumped. She was less prepared for such technicalities, having spent most of her reconditioning time on sprinting. On top of everything else, Marion was competing against her long-jump heroine, Jackie Joyner-Kersee, perhaps the world's greatest woman athlete. Jackie had been Marion's idol since Marion was a little girl and Jackie was winning Olympic gold medals and first places in the seven-event heptathalon.

The two traded leads during each of their six jumps. Marion led first by jumping 22 feet 3 1/4 inches. Jackie's fifth jump of 22 feet 8 inches gave her the lead. Marion gathered her thoughts and nearly flew down the runway. Her takeoff, her airborne form, and her landing were all askew. But when the officials measured, Marion's last jump was 22 feet 9 inches— one inch farther than Jackie's. Marion Jones was the new national long jump champion, breaking Jackie's seven-year hold on the title.

Her two U.S. Championships left no doubt. *Track and Field News Magazine* put Marion on its front cover with the headline, "She's Back!"

Fortune came with her new track fame. Nike signed her to an endorsement contract. The company saw Marion as more than an extraordinary athlete. Besides possessing muscles, she was an attractive woman who could bring new fans to track and field. Her lovely smile gathered admirers faster than her feet ran. People liked to look and listen to her. Sponsored by Nike, she and C.J. would never have to scrape up small change for a pay phone again.

Now the U.S. champion, Marion needed to prove herself against the elite of the world,

Two champions. Marion laughs with 4-time Olympian track and field star Jackie Joyner-Kersee during the U.S. Track and Field Trials for the 2000 Olympics. Kersee's sixth-place finish ended her bid to compete in a fifth consecutive Olympic games.

against more athletes who ran for money as well as titles. Running was now her job, and she had to do her best despite differences in time zones, foods, and unusual starting guns. Meets in Europe taught Marion that she was running faster than she had ever run and that the competition was running fast, too. To win, she had to use her speed, her determination, and her technique to their fullest advantage.

The World Championships at Athens was her biggest test. If she did well there, everyone would know that she was back on track.

Her times improved in each semifinal heat, from 11.03 and 10.96. In the final, she got a great start out of the blocks. Thinking she had left her competitors behind her, Marion relaxed just enough to let the Ukraine's Zhanna Pintusevich challenge her from behind. Marion poured on the speed, leaning forward at the tape. The finish was so close, Zanna began a victory lap, thinking she had won. But the judges reviewed tapes of the finish and found Marion had edged Zanna out, winning her first world championship.

NIKE SHOX

Corporate sponsorship allowed Marion to concentrate on her Olympic training without having to worry about money. Here she brushes up on her basketball skills in a product endorsement for Nike athletic shoes.

Leaving the track with C.J., Marion cried. "It was quick, though," said C.J. "It's Marion—she even cries fast."

Though she didn't make the finals in the long jump, Marion ran with Chryste Gaines, Inger Miller, and Gail Devers to win a first place world championship in the 4x100 relay. She added a pair of World golds to her pair of U.S. medals.

A few weeks later in Brussels, Belgium, Marion shaved .07 seconds off her 100-meter record, taking just 10.76 seconds to complete 47 and a half strides. Track experts and the media called Marion Jones "the fastest woman in the world."

"As long as you're running fast," she said, "life is good."

5

LET'S JUST RACE

Hardly anyone, anywhere in the world, could touch Marion after the starting gun went off.

"I want to run faster than any woman has ever run," Marion said. That meant breaking Florence Griffith Joyner's incredible 10.49 record for 100 meters and 21.34 in the 200. Her times were so spectacular that rumors persisted that Florence had used performance-enhancing drugs or that the wind helped her. Marion dismissed both possibilities.

"The times were legal," Marion said. "The bottom line is that she ran it. And if she ran it, it can be done again."

Marion Jones knew just the person to try. To evaluate her chances in the World Championships and the 2000 Olympics, Marion decided to run against the world's best. Her agent, Charlie Wells, compiled a demanding schedule with 37 events in 27 different meets. Between February and September, she'd go to Australia, then travel to Japan, North Carolina, California, Japan, China, Oregon, Finland, Italy, New Orleans, Austria, Norway, Italy, New

Glowing with victory, Marion shares her joy with a wave to the crowd.

York, Paris, Sweden, Monaco, Switzerland, Belgium, Germany, Russia, and South Africa.

The reward was worth the travel. Marion's statistics lapped the field of competitors. She ran the 100 meters under 11 seconds 18 times. Her times were the sixth fastest in the world. She held the three fastest times in the 200 meters and the three longest jumps in the world. Four months into her schedule she arrived in New Orleans for the U.S. Nationals. Marion won three titles in the 100 meters, the 200 meters, and the long jump. No woman had done that in 50 years. She was ranked number one in all three events.

No wonder her competitors were not happy. "I heard that some of them were saying, 'We're going to get ready for her. We'll have her in '99.' That just motivated me more," said Marion.

Journalists pestered Marion about Christine Arron, whose 100-meter time of 10.73 seconds approached Marion's. Christine had called Marion "arrogant" and the media made the most of it. Was she threatened by Arron's abilities?

"Let's just race," she responded, weary of all the questions.

When the two met in Belgium, Marion easily defeated Arron. In a world of ticks on the clock and widths of skin layers, her 0.15-second margin was huge.

Marion's golden season of 1998 was supposed to climax at the IAAF World Cup Meet in Johannesburg, South Africa. With optimal track conditions there, she hoped to beat Florence Griffith Joyner's record. She finished the 100 meters in 10.65, a personal best and the 200 in 21.62, closer and closer to her goal. But her long jump fell three inches behind Heike Drechsler's.

Despite 1998's other 36 wins, her number one rankings, and her $858,333 prize winnings, all Marion could remember was her last loss to Heike Drechsler. It shamed her.

"I made it a point that I wanted to win my last competition. I wanted to be able to rise above it when my body and my mind were tired, and I felt shot. All I could think about was that long jump and how lousy I competed and how it wasn't me." She vowed not to let that happen again.

Back in the United States, Marion's thoughts turned to wedding dresses and veils. She and C.J. were married October 3 and settled quietly in between Raleigh and Chapel Hill, North Carolina. Their home includes ten acres for Paulie and Izzie, their two dogs. Their life away from the track was low-key. They played H-O-R-S-E in their driveway, watched *The People's Court* and *Judge Judy* on television, or challenged each other in video games. "We just connect," explained C.J. "She's my best friend."

Marion was happy. "I've never in my life had somebody whom I could tell everything to," she said. "Now I have a companion."

Content with her personal and professional life, Marion set new goals for 1999. One was her decision to stay in track "as long as it takes to go after Florence's records." Another was to include the 4x400 relay at the World Championships in Seville, Spain, and then add the 4x100 relay to her Olympic repertoire in Sydney.

"Five golds is not just talk," she announced. "It's possible. If any athlete can do it, it's myself. I was born with a lot of talent, but I'm also a very hard worker."

The number one long jumper in the world still had terrible technique. No matter how

Dressed to the nines, Marion and husband C.J. Hunter step out in style and enjoy a red carpet welcome.

much she practiced, once she started down the runway, anything might happen. She might set a world record or she might disqualify herself. Onlookers had plenty of advice. Get a new coach, a long-jump specialist. Give up jumping entirely. Concentrate on sprint events.

"That just makes me want to come out here and jump, jump, jump and prove them all wrong," Marion said.

Marion took advantage of opportunities to compete, traveling from Oregon to Norway, and then to her practice track in Raleigh. What should have been a pleasant performance on her home turf turned tense and dramatic. The 3,000 spectators were uneasy, watching the world's number one jumper trail Adrien Sawyer, a little-known athlete from Texas. On her last attempt, Marion sped towards the pit and jumped. Marion's jump measured 23 feet, beating Sawyer's best jump by 7 inches. Marion had won the event but almost jeopardized her career. Landing awkwardly in the hard sand, Marion hyperextended her knee. After the pain and swelling subsided, Marion learned she had suffered no permanent damage. But she would spend the crucial training period before the U.S. Nationals on the couch.

Not yet at full strength, Marion arrived at the U.S. Nationals where the unthinkable happened. Another little-known athlete outdistanced Marion by seven inches. It was a stunning defeat. Marion showed another side of a true champion. She scrambled out of the sand, and congratulated the winner, demonstrating an important quality of a true champion. In the press conference later she explained, "I think the true competitor comes out when you act graciously in defeat."

Three days later, Marion was back in top form, winning the 200 meters with a 22.10 finish.

Losing in the long jump didn't change her goal to compete in four events at the World Championships in Seville, Spain. She used the experience to motivate her. "If anything, they've been put into stone," Marion said.

Just before the World Championships, another drug controversy surfaced, diverting media attention from the bright expectations of the competitors to a darker side of sports. Several athletes tested positive for steroid use and were suspended. Random drug tests detected even minuscule amounts sometimes found in harmless cold remedies. Marion always passed her tests. She even avoided sesame and poppy seed bagels (eating these seeds can sometimes result in a false-positive drug test result).

"All I can do is continue to be clean and be around people who are clean," she said. "It's sad, though, isn't it? Everybody wants you to run fast, but once you do, there's suspicion. It's kind of a dead-end road either way."

All eyes were on Marion and C.J. when they arrived in Seville. Everyone expected multiple wins from Marion. So did Marion.

"I'm not coming here to play games," she said. "I will be disappointed if I come back with anything less than four."

The World Championships became a family event. First C.J. threw the shot put 71 feet 6 inches, a personal best and his first international championship win. The next day Marion captured her own gold in the 100 meters with a blistering 10.70 seconds.

Then came that dreaded long jump. With her international arch-rival, Heike Drechsler, out with a calf injury, Marion's chances seemed good. But 22 feet 5 inches was the longest legal jump she could do. Her last try, the best in the meet, was disqualified. The spike on her right foot pierced the plastic boundary. The official waved a red flag. Marion's third place ended her dream of four World wins.

Suffering with back spasms during the 200-meter semifinal in Seville, Spain, Marion drops to her knees. The attack was a crushing defeat for Marion, forcing her to end the 1999 season early.

Her favorite event, the 200 meters, lay ahead. She hadn't lost a 200 in 22 outings. With ten extra seconds and 100 extra meters, it gave Marion more opportunity to run. The staggered lanes allowed Marion to see whom she wanted to outrun. She could accelerate around the track's curve, the centrifugal force releasing her down the straightaway like a slingshot.

But after four 100-meter races and eight long jumps, Marion's body began failing her. An ache. Muscles in her back started to tighten after her qualifying 200 meter heat. A twinge. Massage and acupuncture didn't help. Then pain. Whichever way she moved, it moved with her. By the morning of her semifinal competition, her back muscles were so tight the acupuncture needle couldn't even go in.

Marion knew all she had to do that evening was finish in the top four to qualify for the final. If she could just get down the straightaway to the finish line, she could rest overnight.

At the gun, she got a good start and moved up to lead. At the curve, where she once broke her shoe speeding toward the finish, Marion's tight back muscles wrenched into a full-blown spasm. It was like jamming a stick into bicycle spokes—everything stopped. Marion willed her legs to move. They wouldn't. She fell to the ground, clutching her back. She rolled face-up on the track, her knees in the air. The 40,000 people in the stadium fell silent.

Medics carried her off the track on a gurney. C.J. and Trevor ran to be with her. Big Marion rushed to her side.

Her doctors carefully examined her. She did not have a spinal or a disk injury. Medication eased the spasms. Two and a half hours later, she slowly walked to her ride back to the motel. Marion was disappointed. She cried and fumed and cried some more. "Poor C.J., he got the brunt of it all," she said. "He went across the street to a candy store where they had my favorite kind of sour licorice. And he got ice cream, too. He was so sweet and patient."

Her agent announced she was withdrawing from the World Championships and that she was ending her season. Her hopes for four medals vanished in a split second, just like her victories had always appeared.

People theorized Marion had attempted too much. They blamed the hot weather. They blamed the hard track. Later, doctors found a genetic condition in her spine. They gave her exercises and ultrasound treatments to strengthen her back. Her old rival, Inger Miller, had her own theory. "Everyone thinks she's invincible—she's not."

Over the next eight months, Marion Jones did something she had never done before: she moved slowly, rehabilitating her back. About her Olympic goals, she was very clear.

"I'm going to Sydney entered in five events. I want to win five golds."

6

HIGH FIVE

There was no doubt Marion had healed. For eight months she had worked hard to strengthen her back. In April, she ran a blistering 400-meter race so fast that her time would have won Seville's World Championships. Two weeks later she continued her Olympic hopes, capturing a world record in the 4x200 relay. In July, she won the 100- and 200-meter and long jump at the U.S. Olympic Trials. People began thinking winning five Olympic golds might be possible, at least for Marion Jones.

Having won her first Olympic Gold medal at Sydney in the 100 meters, Marion was on her way to winning more gold medals than any track star had ever attempted. The 200-meter sprint, the long jump, the 4x100 and the 4x400 relays lay ahead.

"I'm glad that I have three days off to kind of enjoy this," she said after her 100-meter win. "Then it's time to refocus. I have to. There's no other thing to do. I have to do it."

But events wouldn't let Marion concentrate on winning her high five. On Tuesday, September 27, less than 48 hours after her gold-medal triumph, she was in the middle of a scandal.

In February 2001 Marion's achievements on the track were honored with three ESPY Awards: Female U.S. Olympic Athlete of the Year, Women's Track and Field Athlete of the Year, and Female Athlete of the Year.

The International Olympic Committee announced that C.J. had flunked four drug tests. Urine tests, taken early in the summer, showed 1000 times the legal limit of nandrolone, an anabolic steroid. Although C.J. wasn't fully recovered from arthroscopic knee surgery three weeks before and was not competing, the controversy was deafening.

When C.J. called a news conference, he and Marion entered together, holding hands. "I am here to show my complete support for my husband," Marion said. "I believe that the legal system will do what it has to do to clear his name."

C.J. claimed that "there wasn't anything anybody could say or do to get me to bring shame on the people I love." He said the steroid came from an iron supplement which he didn't know contained the banned chemical.

His supporters believed him. A mistake was possible, if the steroid were listed simply as an "all natural product" on the label. They argued world athletes would never knowingly take the drug since nandrolone was easily detectable. His critics disagreed, saying that C.J.'s steroid level was so high he would have to have taken it by injection or pill.

Just having someone accused of drug use so near to Marion tarnished her accomplishments, even though her own drug tests were always negative. The questions directed at her were not about her running and jumping, but whether the drug accusations were true.

Gracious, even with rude questions, Marion didn't get mad. She merely said, "I have four more events to do. I need to focus on those events."

Despite the media circus, Marion slipped off her warm up sweats Wednesday and went to work, doing what she does best—competing.

What could have been a difficult day—qualifying for the long jump and the 200-meter race—turned out to be easy. She qualified for the long jump in one try, and breezed through her preliminary heats in the 200-meter race.

If Wednesday had been a bright event, Thursday, September 29 turned absolutely golden. When she stepped out on the track, Marion's ability to block out everything else took over. C.J.'s problems disappeared as she looked down the track.

"All the days my mom would travel four or five hours to a track meet. All the days my brother would pick me on his hide-and-seek team," she said later. "To let one event ruin it? No way. No way."

The 200-meter sprint was always Marion's favorite. And what a joy it was. After the crack of the gun, Marion took off. Her famous legs striding, her arms pumping, she sped to the finish line. No one could keep up with her. She won by 0.43 seconds, the biggest margin since Wilma Rudolph's win 40 years earlier. It was her second victory lap, her second round of applause, a second American flag over her shoulders, another chance for that famous Marion smile to light up the stadium. In the stands, C.J. waited, clapping and cheering. Marion found him and gave him a kiss.

"I don't think anybody doubted me in the sprints," Marion said later. "But my real test will come [in the long jump]. As you all know, I'm here for greater things than just two gold medals. I'm here to prove to myself that it's possible to walk away from Sydney with five."

Friday's long-jump final was a nightmare. It was the same old story. At the end of the runway, she leaned over, swung her arms four times, tapped the track with her foot, took a

Marion receives a kiss of congratulations from husband C.J. Hunter after her 200-meter win at the 2000 Olympics.

deep breath and took off. At the foul line she flung herself into the air, arms reaching, back arching, legs pumping to fall forward into the sand. She couldn't find the foul line without slowing down. She couldn't propel herself through the air without going fast. Her best jump, 22 feet 8 1/2 inches was four inches behind her own season best and three inches short of her rival, Heike Drechsler.

Everything depended on the sixth jump. Just before she took it, Trevor told her, "Just go for it. It's like taking the last shot in basketball. It will be okay if you don't do it."

Thirteen more strides down the runway, one more jump into the sand. She knew it had not been a clean jump. She scrambled out of the sand, waved to the crowd, shrugged, and tried bravely to smile. But her face was a mask of disappointment. Her medal that night was bronze, not gold. She finished third behind Heike Drechsler and Italy's Fiona May.

"The dream for five is not alive," said Jones. "But I don't regret it at all. I had a shot. It just didn't pan out."

Saturday, September 30 didn't begin well. The U.S. 4x100 team was a shambles. Both Inger Miller and Gail Devers, usually team members, withdrew with hamstring injuries. Even one of the replacements, Chryste Gaines, called the last-minute ensemble a "B" team. Gaines, Torrie Edwards, Nanceen Perry, and Marion hadn't practiced handing off the baton they would carry until just before the race.

Transferring the baton makes all the difference. A good hand-off has to be smooth. As one runner finishes her leg of the race, she reaches forward, placing the baton to the next runner who stretches her open hand backward just as she starts running.

The hand-offs between Edwards to Perry and Perry to Jones were awful. Perry had to grab Marion's arm to get the baton to her. As the other runners sped away, crucial hundredths of seconds ticked off. Marion ran full out. But not even her great heart or talented legs could salvage the race. The U.S. team finished behind the Bahamas and Jamaica, barely earning the bronze medal.

"Immediately after the 4x100 I was depressed," recalls Marion. "But as soon as I went on the warm-up track and saw my (1600) teammates sitting there, I knew I had a job to do and forgot about the 4x100."

Most runners were finished for the day and took days recovering from the tremendous physical and emotional energy they expended.

Marion, Heike Drechsler of Germany, and Fiona May of Italy pose with their medals for the women's long jump. Jones earned a bronze for her performance in the event.

Not Marion. Less than two hours later, Marion ran the 4x400, her fifth event in nine days.

Marion ran the third leg of the relay, only her second 400-meter race of the year. Never mind her preference for short sprints. Never mind the pain the longer distance inflicted. Marion dug into the challenge. Her 49.50 sprint gave the U.S. team a 20-meter lead, so large that the last runner, La Tasha Colander-Richardson might have skipped around the track and still won. The victory was sweet. In a full-fledged Olympic competition, the United States had won the relay only once before.

With her teammates, Marion Jones climbed onto the victory stand to receive her fifth Olympic medal. Some said Marion's ambition was to win five *gold* medals. She had not. Others pointed out that no woman in track and field had ever won *five* medals in a single

Olympics. The history books record that undeniable fact.

Marion seemed aware of both thoughts when she said, "I won my individual events, and I still feel in my heart that I could have won the long jump and the 4x100. But overall I have had a very successful Games."

At 24 years old and with an annual income estimated between three and four million dollars, Marion can do just about anything she wants. She can return to the basketball court as a professional. Or she can keep racing the wind.

"I want the chance to break world records," she says. "It will take more than just one Olympic Games. It's going to take more World Championships, more Olympic golds."

Marion Jones has always been on the move. As a schoolgirl, she out-stepped her neighborhood pals. As a teenager, she sped away from her private hurts and authoritative rebellions. As an adult, she streaked towards her personal and well-publicized ambitions.

No question about it—she will be back. Guaranteed. No athlete with as much talent, as much determination, and as much willingness to work towards her goals would ever stop. Marion Jones is a woman who wins. She's hard as nails. She flashes down the track, leaving even the sound of our cheers behind. She'll keep on running and jumping "Swifter, Higher, Stronger," just like great Olympians always do.

1989 . . . . 100 meters 12.01
200 meters 24.06
400 meters 56.73
1990 .100 meters 11.62
200 meters 23.70
400 meters 54.21
Rio Mesa basketball team . . . . .24.5 point average
11 rebounds
California State High School   1) 100 meters
Track and Field titles   1) 200 meters
1991 . . . . .200 meters 22.67
100 meters 11.17
200 meters 22.67
USA Juniors meet . . . . .1) 100 meters
1) 200 meters
National High School Athlete of the Year
U.S. National Track and Field . . . . .6) 100 meters
Championships for   4) 200 meters
WorldChampionships
California State High School . . . . .1) 100 meters
Track and Field titles   1) 200 meters
1992 . . . .
U.S. Olympic trials . . . . .5) 100 meters 11.14
4) 200 meters 22.58
(American Junior Record)
Olympic alternate for 4x100 relay
California State High School . . . . .1) 100 meters
Track and Field titles   1) 200 meters
National High School Athlete of the Year
1993 .400 meters 52.91
Long jump 22'0.5
Thousand Oaks basketball team . . . . .22.8 point average   14.7 rebounds
California's Division I Player of the Year
California State Track and . . . . .1) 100 meters
Field Championships   1) 200 meters
1) Long jump
National High School Athlete of the Year
CIF Player of the Year
Most Valuable Player of Ventura County
1994
University of North Carolina . . . . .14.2 point average 4.1 rebounds
basketball team   3.2 steals   2.8 assists   494 points
(freshman school record)   111 steals
(freshman school record)   NCAA
Championship
ACC Championships . . . . .1) 100 meters 11.67
1) Long jump 20'3.75"
NCAA Outdoor Championships . . . . . . .2) Long jump 22'1.75"
. . . . .6) 200 meters
1995
University of North Carolina . . . . .17.9 points average   5.0 rebounds
basketball team   4.5 assists   124 steals   628 point
(freshman/sophomore record for
1000 points)

ACC Championships . . . . .1) Long jump 20'10.5"
NCAA Championships . . . . .4) Long jump
1996 . . . . .Did not compete because of injuries
1997
Florida Invitational . . . . .1) 100 meters 11.37
1) Long jump 21'8"
Carolina Invitational . . . . .1) 100 meters 11.19
Tennessee Invitational . . . . .1) 100 meters 10.98
U.S. Nationals . . . . .1) 100 meters 10:97
1) Long jump 22'9"
World Championships . . . . .1) 100 meters 10.83
10) Long jump 21'9"
1) 4x100 meter relay 41.47
(American Record)
1998
Chengdu, China . . . . .1) 100 meters 10.71
U.S. Nationals . . . . .1) 100 meters 10.72
1) 200 meters 22.24
1) Long jump 23'8"
World Championships . . . . .1) 100 meters 10.83
1) U.S. 4x100 relay
IAAF World Cup . . . . .1) 100 meters 10.65 (personal record)
1) 200 meters 21.62 (personal record)
2) Long jump 22 '11.75"
U.S. Nationals . . . . .1) 100 meters 10.72
1) 200 meters 22.24
1) Long jump 23' 8"
Goodwill Games . . . . .1) 100 meters 10.90
1) 200 meters 21.80   Won 35–36
competitions in 1998
1999
Pontiac Grand Prix Invitational . . . . . .1) Long jump 23'0"
U.S. Nationals . . . . .1) 100 meters—Did not compete
1) 200 meters 22.10
2) Long jump 22'3"
World Championships . . . . .1) 100 meters 10.70
3) Long jump 22.5 200 meters—
did not finish
2000
Penn Relays . . . . .1) 4x200 relay 1:27:46 (world record)
Mt. San Antonio College Relays . . . . . .1) 400 meters 49.59
Olympic Trials . . . . .1) 100 meters 10.88
1) 200 meters 21.94
1) Long jump 23'.05"
Olympics . . . . .1) 100 meters 10.75
1) 200 meters 21.84
1) 4x400 meter relay
3) Long jump 22'8 8'4"
3) 4x100 meter relay

CHRONOLOGY

1975	Marion is born October 12.
1977	Marion's mother divorces her father, George Jones.
1983	Marion's mother marries Ira Toler.
1985	Marion begins running track competitively.
1987	Marion's stepfather, Ira Toler, dies of a stroke.
1990	Marion wins state titles in both the 100 and 200 meters. She joins the basketball team, averaging 25 points per game. She wins her first National High School Athlete of the Year award.
1991	Marion runs the 200 meters in 22.87 seconds, breaking the national high school record. She is named the High School Athlete of the Year. At the U.S. Olympic Trials, Marion misses qualifying for the 200 meters by .07. She declines a spot as an alternate in the 4x100 relay for the Barcelona Olympics.
1992	Marion is again named High School Athlete of the Year.
1993	Marion discovers the long jump. In a post office mix-up, she is suspended by the TAC for missing a mandatory drug test and then is cleared. She sets the national high school record in the 200 meters and is named High School Athlete of the Year again.
1994	Marion enrolls at University of North Carolina. She leads the Lady Tar Heels to a National Collegiate Athletic Association (NCAA) Championship. She sets freshman records for points and steals.
1995	In August and December Marion breaks her left foot, missing the 1996 Olympics and her basketball season.
1996	Marion begins a romance with C.J. Hunter. She turns professional as a track athlete.
1997	In May, Marion graduates with journalism and mass communication degree and retrains for a track career. Trevor Graham becomes her coach. In June, she wins U.S.A. Track & Field Outdoor Championships in 100-meter dash (10.90) and the long jump, beating Jackie Joyner-Kersee (Olympic gold medalist and national champion) with a jump of 22'9". In August, Marion wins the 100-meter sprint with a time of 10.76 at the Track and Field World Championships in Athens, Greece. She claims a second medal with the 4x100 relay team.
1998	Marion makes public her intention to try to win five gold medals at the Sydney Olympics. In June, Marion medals in the 100-meter, 200-meter, and long jump events at the U.S. Track and Field Championships. She is the first person in fifty years to do so. In September, Marion takes the 100- and 200-meter titles at the World Cup in Johannesburg, South Africa, with times of 10.65 and 21.62. She is beaten by Heike Drechsler in the long jump, her only loss in 37 events. Marion marries C.J. Hunter October 3.
1999	Her bid for four golds at World Championships in Seville, Spain, ends with a 100-meter win. She takes a bronze in the long jump. Back spasms during the 200-meter semifinal force her to end her season.
2000	In July, Marion wins the 100 meters, 200 meters, and long jump at the U.S. Olympic Trials. Her participation in a 4x200 relay sets a world record. She runs an astonishing 49.59 in the 400-meter race. Her Olympic activities in Sydney, Australia include: September 23 Wins gold in 100-meter sprint September 27 C.J. and Marion defend his failed drug tests September 28 Marion wins gold in the 200-meter sprint September 29 Marion wins bronze in the long jump event September 30 Marion wins bronze with the 4x100 relay; wins gold in the 4x400 relay Marion is named The Associated Press' Female Athlete of the Year.
2001	Marion is named *Track & Field* News 2001 Woman of the Year.

INDEX

FURTHER READING

Gutman, Bill. *Marion Jones: The Fastest Woman in the World.* New York: Pocket Books, 2000.

Rapoport, Ron. *See How She Runs.* Chapel Hill: Algonquin Books, 2000.

Stewart, Mark. *Marion Jones: Sprinting Sensation.* Children's Press, 2000.

Wallechinsky, David. *The Complete Book of Summer Olympics.* Sydney: Overlook Press, 2000.

Wickham, Martha. *Superstars of Women's Track and Field.* Philadelphia: Chelsea House Publishers, 1997.

ABOUT THE AUTHOR

VICKI COX is a freelance feature writer for national magazines and newspapers in 16 states. Her anthology of stories, *Rising Stars and Ozark Constellations,* was published in 2001. Ms. Cox has an M.S. in education and taught for 25 years. She speaks at writer and education conferences. She lives in Lebanon, Missouri.

HANNAH STORM, NBC Sports play-by-play announcer, reporter, and studio host, made her debut in 1992 at Wimbledon during the All England Tennis Championships. Shortly thereafter, she was paired with Jim Lampley to cohost the *Olympic Show* for the 1992 Olympic Games in Barcelona. Later that year, Storm was named cohost of *Notre Dame Saturday,* NBC's college football pregame show. Adding to her repertoire, Storm became a reporter for the 1994 Major League All-Star Game and the pregame host for the 1995, 1997, and 1999 World Series. Storm's success as host of *NBA Showtime* during the 1997–98 season won her the role as studio host for the inaugural season of the Women's National Basketball Association in 1998.

In 1996, Storm was selected as NBC's host for the Summer Olympics in Atlanta, and she has been named as host for both the 2000 Summer Olympics in Sydney and the 2002 Winter Olympics in Salt Lake City. Storm received a Gracie Allen Award for Outstanding Personal Achievement, which was presented by the American Women in Radio and Television Foundation (AWRTF), for her coverage of the 1999 NBA Finals and 1999 World Series. She has been married to NBC Sports broadcaster Dan Hicks since 1994. They have two daughters.